LOCOMOTIVES INTERNATIONAL

PICTORIAL REVIEW No. 1

BULGARIA

BDŽ 03.12 approaching a ruin at 08:55 on the morning of Sunday, October 23, 2022, near Momchilgrad.

BDŽ 16.27 powered a special train from Kyustendil to Gyueshevo, on October 28, 2022. This view was recorded at 08:13 (just a few moments after sunrise) on the north side of Kyustendil.

In a scene reminiscent of a cool, clear, South African winter morning, at 08:45 on the morning of October 26, 2022, BDŽ 609.76 is seen departing Dobrinishte

On October 25, 2022, BDŽ 609.76 performed a runpast at the small station named Pashovo, now disused. In the field across the railway line from the station is a small apple orchard.

All: Thomas R Schultz

Charter train with 609.76, having started at the bottom of the line at Dobrinishte, piloted by Henschel diesel 75006 for the last leg of the journey to the summit of the line at Avromovo. The diesel was added at Yakoruda, and seen here at Cherna Mesta on 26th October 2022.

At rest at Kyustendil station on 27th October 2022, having worked the charter train from Radomir, 16.27 – a 2-10-0 of German type 42, built in Floridsdorf (Vienna) c.1949, in readiness for the continuation of the special train to Gyushevo the next day.

2-10-0 16.27 and train arriving at the designated photo spot, shortly after sunrise on 28th October 2022.

12. 16.27 finally arrives at Gyushevo in the late afternoon at the end of its 45km journey.

All: Vic Allen

CZECH REPUBLIC

555.0153 (ex DR class 42 Kriegslok) pulls away from Straskov with the Praha – Žatec leg of the IGEG 40th anniversary railtour on 7th September 2022.

OBB 77.28 departs Postupice with the 0946 Benešov – Trhový Štěpánov, 10th September 2022.

An Austrian themed line up at Benešov depot on the evening of 10th September. Left to Right: OBB 77.28, CSD 354.7152, OBB 310.23 (renumbered as CSD 375.007), CSD 434.2187.

OBB 77.26, CSD 354.7152 & CSD 375.007 await the next day's action, Benešov shed, 10th September 2022.

All: Bryan Acford

FRANCE

The majestic Viaduc du Viaur is situated on the railway line from Toulouse via Carmaux to Rodez. To mark its 120th anniversary, a steam train hauled by 141 R 1126 ran on 4th September 2022 from Toulouse over the viaduct to Naucelle. it is seen (*above*) at Roqueserière-Buzet, and (*below*) on the Viaduct (note the standby diesel at the back of the train).

Both: Ad van Sten

GERMANY

A piece of railway romance is coming to an end. The last double telegraph poles (the so-called H-poles) in Germany between Cottbus and Görlitz have disappeared. To mark the occasion, a group of railway enthusiasts organised several trips on this former main line on 20 and 21 April 2022, with the freshly overhauled 03 2255-4 and a wonderful looking express train. Here it is near Kodersdorf.

From 28th April until 1st May steam trains returned to Usedom, Germany's most northeastern Baltic Sea island. # 86 1333-3 (WLF Floridsdorf No. 3211/1939) ran as 86 1759-9 (one of the locomotives once stationed at Usedom) four times a day between the seaside resort of Heringsdorf and Zinnowitz. We see it leaving Heringsdorf.

Both: Ad van Sten

To conclude its 40th anniversary celebrations, German railtour operator IGE organised a special event on 10th September 2022, based on the fierce 7km 1 in 40 Schiefe Ebene ramp. This involved eleven separate trains featuring seven locomotives in different formations, single or double-headed, many with a steam banker. Above are 44.2456 with 52.8195 banking, and below 01.0509-8 & 01.519, again with 52.8195 banking.

Both: Dave Collier

A special trip on 1st October may have been the last run of 001 180-9, the only operable 01 with a new high-performance boiler. An upcoming general overhaul is planned, but it is doubtful whether this will be carried out. The train started in Nördlingen in south Bavaria and went from Nuremberg via the Pegnitz valley with no less than seven tunnels and Bayreuth to the Steam Locomotive Museum in Neuenmarkt-Wirsberg. Both pictures show the train near Löpsingen.

Both: Ad van Sten

A journey on the 5.6km Woltersdorfer Strassenbahn was enjoyed on 24th September 2022, particularly as the 60 year old trams were soon to be replaced by modern efficient vehicles. Tram 32 has arrived at Woltersdorf.

At the Dresden Dampflok celebrations on 23rd September 2022, immaculate class 52 2-10-0 52.8141 is moving on to the turntable before being exhibited to the audience from all angles as the turntable rotates. Note the Giesl exhaust arrangements, which gave the locomotive a very crisp exhaust sound, when it hauled one of the special trains later in the weekend.

Both:David Knapman

0-4-4-0T 99 1542-2 departing from Steinbach on the Pressnitztalbahn on 4th December 2022.

2-10-2T 99 1793-1 with the 09.25 Freital - Hainsberg to Kipsdorf train on the Weisseritzalbahn on 2nd December 2022.

Both: David Gillis

Rasender Roland's summer timetable, which runs through to the end of October, sees several trains running after dark. 2-8-0T 99 4802-7 waits for time at Göhren. Its train, the 19:53, took it through to Putbus where its day ended. 09 October 2022.

Former Kleinbahnen des Kreises Jerichow I 2-8-0T 99 4802-7 between Sellin Ost and Sellin West with the 09:53 from Göhren to Lauterbach Mole. This was an unusual duty for the locomotive at this time, later in the day it was swapped back to its normal diagram during a cross with 99 783 at Binz LB. 12 October 2022.

2-10-2T 99 783 is one of the high season regulars at Rasender Roland (the Rügensche BäderBahn). Here, this one time resident of Saxony, accelerates away from Sellin Ost. It was at the head of the 11:53 from Göhren to Lauterbach Mole. 12 October 2022.

All: Martyn Bane

Same crossing - different views! The upper view shows 99.236 at Steinerne Renne on the Harzquerbahn on 6th January 2023. Moving a short distance gives the alternative view below of 99.7241-5 on the same date.

Both: Dave Collier

99 234 hauls the Harzer Schmalspurbahn's 08:55 from Wernigerode to Brocken up the 1 in 30 gradient close to Drei Annen Gasthaus. Along with much of the area, this part of the Drängetal has been cleared of trees in recent years. 03 January 2023.

99 7240-7 near the summit of the Broken with the 13:39 from Drei Annen Hohne. Torfhaus transmitters, once in West Germany, are in the distance, much lower down. 03 January 2023.

Both: Martyn Bane

52.7596 crosses the Tennetschlutch viaduct, Langenbrand on the Murg Valley Railway with a railtour en route to Baiersbronn on 18th February 2023.

Compound S 3/6 No 3673 of 1918, seen here just after dawn passing over the river Worntiz beneath Harburg Castle heading for Donauworth at the head of the eleven coach Bayerisches Eisenbahnmuseum railtour on 25th February, unassisted.

Sunrise over the river Regnitz at Furth on the outskirts of Nuremberg as the IGE 40th Anniversary tour starts Day 2 behind the two Pacifics 01.202 & 01.519, heading for Saalfeld. 27th February 2023.

After Saalfeld the loco composition on the 6-coach train was changed so that 01.202 was leading while 01.519 brought up the rear tender-first. This facilitated the change in direction for the train after Arnstadt. The consist is seen here near Paulinzella, heading for Arnstadt.

All: Dave Collier

HUNGARY

On 13 and 14 August, a so-called retro-train event took place along Lake Balaton. In addition to classic diesel locomotives, steam locomotive 424.247 was also involved, albeit only on the Saturday. It is seen (*above*) passing Örvényes station, and (*below*) west of Révfülöp.

Both: Ad van Sten

ITALY

The only FS class 880 locomotive currently in steam is 880.001, owned by the Associazione Società Veneta Ferrovie (SVF) in Primolano, where it is occasionally steamed with two matching coaches (a two-axle type 1936 and a so-called Corbellini from 1952) and two goods wagons. These pictures were taken during such an event on 8th October 2022.

Both: Ad van Sten

On 8th May 2022, 2-6-0 no. 625.017 (Ansaldo 898/1910) hauled the Treno Natura (Nature Train) from Siena (*above*), via Buonconvento, to Monte Antico, where the train reversed and continued to Asciano Scalo (*below*).

Pistoia depot is now the main collecting and storage centre in Tuscany and is amassing a large collection of locomotives for restoration and display. 2-8-0 no. 740.244 stands (*above*) on 7th May 2022. (*Below*) Unrestored Crosti boilered Class 2-8-0 no. 741.120 on 7th May 2022.

All: David Gillis

23

A 2TE116UM twin unit heads north near Bayan with a container train from China. 14th August 2022.

In early morning light, a 2TE25KM twin unit snakes along the Khoolt pass, north towards Ulaanbaatar. 16th August 2022.

A 2TE25KM twin unit lead an iron ore train on the northern approaches of Ulaanbaatar. 17th August 2022.

With the Khentii mountains in the distance, a 2TE25KM twin unit with empty containers for China heads south long the Kharra river valley north of Ulaanbaatar. 19th August 2022.

All photographs by Gary Thomas

A Russian bound mixed train, headed by 2TE116UM twin unit heads along with Kharra river valley north of Ulaanbaatar. 19th August 2022.

A local passenger train, led by a 2TE116UM twin unit arrives at Tunkh with a train to Ulaanbaatar. Tunkh is a popular tourist destination for Mongolians. 20th August 2022.

An M62 leads a Ulaanbaatar bound train south from Tunkh. 20th August 2022.

An M62 departs Ulaanbaatar with a passenger train for Russia made up of Russian stock. A significant amount of marshalling happens in the yard to the right. 21st August 2022.

All photographs by Gary Thomas

NETHERLANDS

Currently there are only two operable NS steam locomotives left in the Netherlands. One of them is 8107, owned by the Museum Buurtspoorweg (MBS) in Haaksbergen. Under ideal conditions, this engine was used on 5th November 2022 to travel back in time to the 1930s, partly with the help of some road vehicles and actors (even with matching hairstyles). Both the passenger and goods train had been put together with the utmost care. The results are on these pages...

All: Ad van Sten

NEW ZEALAND

On 16th October 2022 the Glenbrook Vintage Railway (GVR) celebrated the centenary of the opening of the Waiuku Branch line, which officially opened on 5th January 1922 and the inaugural train was hauled by two Ww class locomotives hauling sixteen carriages. Ww644 & 480 head the re-enactment train past Shakespeare Road on the GVR.

Ja 1271 hauls a celebratory excursion returning to Auckland at Helvetia, located on the rebuilt section of the Waiuku branch between Paerata and Glenbrook.

DBR 1295 & 1254 head the empty stock working for the excursion back to Auckland along the GVR at Victoria Avenue, Waiuku.

The relaunched 'Kingston Flyer' passed Fairlight on 26th February 2023 behind Ab795.

All: Robert Sweet

To mark forty years since the opening of the Museum of Transport & Technology's (MOTAT) railway at the Keith Park Memorial Airfield on Meola Road in 1982 all three current operating steam locomotives were in operation for the monthly rail operating day on 20th November 2022. The railway ran two mixed trains which ran between the two station sites in the MOTAT complex. Each mixed train was top and tailed by a British built locomotive. The all steam mixed train (*above*) had L 507 (Avonside Engineering Co. of 1877) leading and F 180 (Yorkshire Engine Co. of 1880) at the rear. The steam and diesel mixed train (*below*) had Y 542 (Hunslet Engine Co of 1923) leading with Dsa 223 (Drewry/Vulcan of 1953) at the rear.

A close up of F 180.

Y 542 and F 180 pass in the station area at MOTAT.

All: Robert Sweet

As part of Steam Incorporated's 50th birthday celebrations this year the Glenbrook Vintage Railway (GVR) joined up with Steam Incorporated to run a triple headed 20 vehicle excursion train billed as "Mountain Thunder" from Palmerston North to Raurimu and return on 6th August 2022. The train consisted of 13 Steam Incorporated red carriages plus GVR's 6 yellow carriages and AG generator van and was sold out with 800 passengers on board. Motive power was GVR's DBR 1254 (built 1965 by GMD, London, Ontario, Canada as Db 1005 and rebuilt 1981 as DBR 1254 by Clyde Engineering, Rosewater, South Australia) plus

Steam Incorporated's Da 1410 (built 1955 by GMD, London, Ontario, Canada) and 1431 (built 1957 by Clyde Engineering, Granville, NSW, Australia). The train is seen (*from above left*) at Cliff Road; crossing Makatote Viaduct; rounding the curve at Taihape; and passing Mangaweka.

All: Robert Sweet

On a visit to Wolsztyn on 2nd and 3rd November 2022, our photographer was fortunate to capture Ol49-69 in service for the final time before entering the sheds at Wolsztyn for repairs, which were still ongoing in August 2023.

All: Ad van Sten

PORTUGAL

After an absence of more than a year, narrow gauge loco E 214 ran Christmas trains on the Vouga railway line from Aveiro via Macinhata do Vouga to Sernada do Vouga on 10/11th and 17/18th December 2022. It is pictured at Cabanões and crossing the Vouga bridge near Sernada do Vouga.

Both: Ad van Sten

Ex. SS 2-8-4T No. 0186 waits to cross a service train in Pinhao station whilst working the Tua - Regua return leg of the "Douro Historical Train" on 24th September 2022.

Ex. PPF 0-6-0T No. 6 "Povoa De Varzim" and ex. CFG 2-6-0T No. 6 "Soares Velloso" stand inside the railway museum at Lousado on 29th September 2022.

Both: David Cox

764.480 approaches Novicor on the CFF Viseu de Sus with a train of empty logging bogies during a Farrail Tour on 6th February 2023.

764.431 pulls well tank 764.159 out of the loco-shed at Moldovița on 8th February 2023.

On the same day 764.431 passes some traditional Romanian rural transport between Râșca and Argel with empty logging bogies heading for the current terminus of the line at Argel.

All: Bryan Acford

SOUTH AFRICA

A photo charter was operated by the Ceres Railway over the impressive Michell's Pass between Prince Alfred Hamlet, Ceres and Wolseley in South Africa from 16 to 18 June 2022. The locomotive in charge was 19B 1412 and, on the last day, the oil-fired 19D 3321. From top left: the two locomotives are seen in Demeter station, Ceres, at the start of the day on 16th; 1412 approaches Wolseley; 1412 passes through the Michell's Pass, and; 3321 departs from Demeter on 18th.

All: Ad van Sten

SWEDEN

On 3rd December 2022, a small group of railway photographers chartered the S1 1914 for a run from Brösarp to Sankt Olof. In the evening the engine was joined in Brösarp yard by E2 1183, which was in steam as well (*below*).

All: Ad van Sten

On 24th September 2022, the Inlandsbanan, which runs northwards from Kristinehamn to Mora and up the centre of Sweden to Gällivare above the Arctic Circle, 1288 Km in length, celebrated the 100th anniversary of the completion of track between Sveg and Brunflo near Östersund. A special steam-hauled train was operated from Östersund to Överhogdal, where the line had originally been completed, a distance of 130 Km. The train was hauled by SJ 0-8-0 No E2 904 built in 1907, owned by the

Swedish Railway Museum at Gävle, who also provided the stock. From above left: Lockne nr Brunflo; in the forest nr Sortjarn; journey's end and celebrations underway, and; on the return journey at Strombacka, Hackås.

All: Dave Collier

SWITZERLAND

The Rorschach-Heiden-Bergbahn is a railway line that starts at Lake Constance. The former operating company of the same name, abbreviated to RHB, was absorbed by the Appenzeller Bahnen (AB) in 2006. The line built by the RHB is a 5.60 kilometer standard gauge rack railway from Rorschach on Lake Constance to Heiden, which is almost 400 meters higher. Here we see the trackwork at Heiden station, including points with Riggenbach rack rails. In the background is ABDeh 2/4 AB 23 (SLM/BBC /1953) on 10th August 2022.

Tmh 2/2 AB 20 (SLM/BBC /1962) (ex Sulzer 4, KUMA Thm 237 916) at Rorschach depot.

The Frauenfeld-Wil Bahn is a 1,000 mm gauge railway line in Switzerland, which connects the town of Frauenfeld in the canton Thurgau to the town of Wil in the canton of St. Gallen, following the valley of the Murg river. The Frauenfeld-Wil-Bahn (FWB) opened the line in 1887 and operated it until 2021, when that company merged into Appenzeller Bahnen (AP). The line is nowadays included in Tarifverbund Ostwind, and operates as service S15 of the St.Gallen S-Bahn. In 2011 railway company ordered five new ABe4/8 low floor trains from Stadler Rail. Here we see car 5 at Wil on 16th August 2022.

All: Uwe Pietruck

TURKEY

56149 plinthed at Kara Tren Parki, Efeler, Aydin on 1st July 2022.

600mm gauge 97 plinthed outside Alsancak station in Izmir on 1st July 2022.

Left to right from the top of 56045. 45172, 45132, 45002, 46005, 56712, 3705, 46059, 4, 57026, 34056, 57018, 44041, 138, 46025, 56130 and 5701 at Camlik museum on 1st July 2022.

44062 stored at Alsancak Depot on 1st July 2022.

All: David Gillis

UKRAINE

In early July 2022, the contents of the railway museum at Antonivka were evacuated by special standard gauge train to Korostiv, as seen in these pictures.

Both: Wolfram Wendelin

The Grand Canyon Railroad runs a daily train from Williams to Canyon Village at the Grand Canyon South Rim. The 1520 Canyon Village – Williams train leaves Canyon village on 14th October 2022 headed by GP40 237 + 4128.

Former Manitou & Pikes Peak Railway No 4 on display at Williams.

Both: Bryan Acford

During the first two weeks of February, the impressive 2-6-6-2 Mallet #1309 ran five trips with a freight train between Cumberland, MD and Frostburg in her authentic Chesapeake and Ohio livery. Whether this can ever be repeated seems very unlikely. Meanwhile, the locomotive has been painted back to Western Maryland Scenic Railroad colours. It is just a name, but a world of difference. The formation is pictured (*from top left*) at Cumberland; rounding the Helmstetter curve; leaving the Brush Tunnel; and at Frostburg.

All: Ad van Sten

Two eastbound freights waiting at Cheyenne, Wyoming on 2nd July 2022. On the left, a mixed consist headed by seven EMD & GE locos lead by GE ES44AH number 2546. The seventh loco is an EMD SD70 belonging to the Kansas City Southern Railroad. On the right, a special train of wind turbine parts, headed by EMD SD70AH number 8996 and two GE ES44s, has paused to change crew.

Bringing up the rear of an Amtrak Hiawatha service to Milwaukee at North Canal Street level crossing in Chicago is a driving trailer no. 90221, one of 22 rebuilt from F40PH locos and finished in a special livery saluting America's military veterans. These cars are known as "Cabbage" cars since they combine a driving cab with a baggage section. 20th June 2022.

Both: Kevin Hoggett